HOW
TO LOOK GOOD IN PHOTOS

by

Kate Branch

About the author.

Kate Branch is a portrait photographer based in North Sydney, Australia. Kate majored in photography at the University of New South Wales.

Kate also received photographic training from her father, a former photojournalist and advertising photographer for Ogilvy & Mather. Kate was taught how to take a photograph before learning how to drive a car.

Kate completed her masters in Art Therapy at the University of Western Sydney.

First Printing, 2014

National Library of Australia Cataloguing-in-Publication entry:

Author: Branch, Kate, author.
Title: How to look good in photos : his and hers tips and tricks / Kate Branch

ISBN: 9780992513207 (paperback)
Subjects: Portrait photography--Posing.
             Portrait photography--Lighting.
Dewey Number: 778.92

Kate Branch Publishing
5/89 Ridge St, North Sydney, Australia, 2060
www.katebranch.com

Time it was, and what a time it was, it was
A time of innocence, a time of confidences
Long ago, it must be, I have a photograph
Preserve your memories, they're all that's left you.

Simon& Garfunkel

$\mathcal{D}$EDICATION

For Jean-Claude and Sophia,
Thank you for all the support you have given me.
Words cannot explain how much I love you,
But my photos can.

TABLE OF CONTENTS

$\mathscr{I}$NTRODUCTION

$\mathscr{H}$aving your picture taken can be daunting. All your little insecurities come out to play. We may be insecure about our stomach so we stand behind people with our arms crossed in every picture. We may be insecure about or teeth so we never open our mouth and always look a little grim.

The most common posing mistakes I have experienced when photographing clients are:

- Covering their mouth with their hand as they are ashamed of bad teeth.
- Crossing their hands in front of their body as they are unhappy with their stomach.
- Throwing their hands in front of their face and saying, "No photos, please."
- Making a funny face such as sticking out their tongue because they are anxious.

The only problem is if we cover up our insecurities incorrectly, we never will have a nice picture of ourselves. It's okay to have insecurities. We all have them. But if we tackle them correctly we also can enjoy nice images of ourselves. Posing can be like an amazing concealer, it can cover all the unwanted lumps and bumps if we know how.

However, we have to identify our insecurities before we can have a nice photograph of ourselves taken.

When I was younger, I always would tilt my head to the right whenever I saw a camera. It often looked like I had dislocated my head. But somewhere along the line, I decided this looked good and posed this way for every photograph. It was a posing defence. I even remember a particularly critical girl at school saying, "You look so funny when you do that," and I became even more insecure. But I kept doing it. I detested having my picture taken at this stage.

Looking back, I know why I did it. I never liked my smile. I had a very crooked smile as a child. My teeth were crooked until I had braces, but even once they were straight I still was not happy. My teeth are bigger than usual and when I was younger I was embarrassed by that. So I thought if I tilted my head it would distract the attention away from my smile. (I just looked uncomfortable in the process). Defensive actions rarely have logic applied to them.

Luckily when I was training in photography, a colleague was running some test shots at night. Reluctantly, I stood in front of my colleague as she tested the flash. When she showed me the result, I was gobsmacked. The flash had completely blown out all the detail in my smile. I finally loved a picture of myself, and I felt much better. No more weird head tilting! And can you believe that as an extremely shy girl, I grew into a confident lady who went on to dabble in modelling? Representing my country as Miss Australia World University in South Korea, Miss Australia Queen of the World in Europe, and Miss Australia World Cup as well as modelling for Porsche in Germany. It was a milestone for me and worlds apart from where I first began. I have since graced magazine covers and I enjoy posing for photo shoots. So the proof is in the pudding.

BEFORE: I was always nervous in front of the camera. I created a head tilt that I believed compensated for my large, crooked teeth. A lot of people who are never educated in how to present for the camera have a nervous defence mechanism.

AFTER: The first image is me on the cover of North side magazine. The following images were captured by my husband, my wedding photographer Nathan Weymark, or are self portraits.

From that moment on, I stopped focusing on photography books and directed my attention to experimenting with my clients. What made their arms look thinner? How could I reduce their wrinkles (my favourite these days)? How could I accommodate someone nervous about their tummy?

In today's world you would have to be a recluse to avoid a camera. Everywhere I go I see someone capturing a moment with a camera phone. Never has it been a more appropriate time to be photogenic. And it is not even an issue of vanity. Below is a list of some of the reasons why people need photographs of themselves:

-Your own website, if you run a small business.
-C.V.'s are getting noticed by placing a headshot in the corner.
-Dating websites.
-Wedding photographs are so expensive people want to look their best.
-Every family memory from this decade forward will be recorded by every individual attending that function, whether you have makeup on or not!

I don't see any of these situations happening due to vanity. We are such a visually-based culture that, more and more, we are leaning on photographs to express, explain, and share our experiences. People want to see you. So say, "Cheese!" Your dream career or dream partner could depend on it.

A client of mine once called for some dating photographs. She was nervous and felt a little silly organising a photo shoot. I simple explained to her that it was not silly, but smart. You want your photograph to stand out. People you are trying to attract see many different profiles. You want to be appealing, interesting and warm.

Do remember that if you're not going to do your best, there will be another clever individual out there who will. And they might get your date! People are no less visual on online dating services than they are seeing each other in a bar.

Another client came to me for some photographs to bring her spirits up. She has been unemployed from the IT industry for six months and said she was feeling depressed. Her sister was getting married and she was watching all these wonderful things happen to her. My client just wanted to feel special for one day. She had brought along girly clothes to shoot at the beach. I stopped her right there. Why don't we do a photo shoot that looks more professional and she could place it on the top of her C.V.? She would still look great, but the images would be put to good use. I gave her my blazer I was wearing and we headed into the financial district. This reset her confidence and vision and her successful C.V. looked amazing.

I am not here to promise falsehoods. I am not saying read this book and you will look like a supermodel. But if you read this book and utilise my tips and tricks- you will look good. These two previous women I discussed were not fashion model-thin (those women look too hungry anyway) but they looked great.

If we want to be inspired by celebrities and models, look at their wedding photos and public appearances. Then you will see their favourite poses and their best angles, the ones they use in real life.

Posing is a tool you can utilise anywhere. It's free and instant. You may not have a couture gown (or you may if it's your wedding) but you will be able to jump into what I call the "slim and streamlined pose" in three seconds. Then, just like the celebrities, you can add hair and makeup or a suit jacket. And voilà! Marilyn Monroe and James Bond- watch out! You have a picture of yourself that will make you want to frame it, post it, and send it out on a Christmas card.

It may take a little bit of time. You are about to step out of your comfort zone. It will take practise, either in front of the mirror or setting the timer on your camera phone. But trust me, it's worth it. I did it myself.

I have taught these tips in workshops. I have had clients ranging from eighteen to eighty. I have had women recovering from breast cancer, and both genders starting businesses, and wanting to date. And there is one truth in all of it. The mass media is making everyone feel bad: pretty teenagers, aging mothers, attractive businessmen, and fiercely independent females.

The proudest career moments are when someone says to me, "That is the best photograph of me ever taken." Or when a student walks out of my class saying, "I wish I had done this earlier. That was great." I have wanted to write this book ever since I worked out the magic of getting a photograph right.

I believe the relationship you have with the camera is similar to the one you have with others and yourself. The camera is just an observer. If you are obsessed with Photoshopping yourself to bits and only sharing photographs of yourself shopping and being fabulous- I wonder how confident you truly are. On the other end of the spectrum, if you hate your photos and only marvel at images of others then that's not a good place to be either.

What we want is a happy medium. Be confident in front of the camera, but also be aware that photos are not everything. They are solely meant to be a memory of your life, not your entire reason for being. I was incredibly shy and that showed in pictures. Now I hope you see a warm and happy face, because that's how I feel. And I would like you to have that feeling, too.

Thank you and enjoy the transformation,
Kate Branch, December 2013

You don't take a photograph, you make it.

Ansel Adams

SLIM AND STREAMLINED POSE

13/ SLIM AND STREAMLINED POSE

*O*nce I was photographing a family portrait. I met the family at the beach and directed them to the best place to pose. The father and his two daughters walked over to the location. The mother just stood closer to me and said, "Oh, I will get in next year's portrait. I'm too large at the moment. I don't want my picture taken."

I empathised with the woman. I have many good friends who battle weight issues. Not only do they have this inner struggle, but they also scrutinise themselves in front of mirrors and in pictures of themselves. Sometimes someone with a weight issue may go years without being in a family picture.

I asked my portrait client how she would feel if I showed her how to look thinner. I explained that the way you stand can highlight your positives and hide your negatives- and it is instant, costs nothing, and does not need hours of preparation.

With her family begging her, and me suggesting a solution, we got a beautiful family picture. My client framed the photograph and proudly says it is showcased in their lounge room. She was thrilled because she had not had a picture with her and her daughters in five years.

You may not have a weight issue yourself. But I know even the healthiest girls and boys have deleted an unflattering photograph of themselves. The camera can be cruel, no matter what your weight. So let's show our best possible figure!

Many people stand facing toward the camera. What they don't realise is this allows the camera to document your complete width. It outlines your figure in the most unflattering light. It presents your width in all its glory, and does not create the most flattering silhouette.

To fix this issue we can learn a lot from diet ads, without having to touch a carrot stick, or run a marathon! If you have a closer look at diet ads, you will see a before and after photo.

Nine times out of ten they have made the subject stand facing forward in the before photo, and have shifted the person's body position for the second image.

So if you want to appear thinner, option one is shifting your weight onto your front foot, bending your back leg slightly. Option two is distributing your weight on your back foot, and resting your front foot pointing towards the camera. Sometimes both options leave people nearly falling over due to feeling unbalanced. If so, the third option is distributing your weight evenly, but making sure you turn to the side. This automatically creates a thinner appearance.

Another problem area people are not happy with is their arms. This is because they are on show for most of the warmer months. A tummy you can hide, a bottom you can cover- but arms have to perform three shows a day for an entire season.

Many people stand with their arms unconsciously squished to their sides. This action makes your arms look much thicker than they actually are. So, by standing self-consciously, you are in fact making your arms look bigger.

Also, don't pose with shoulders square on. Shoulders are the widest part of the body. Shooting straight on is not flattering. Angle the shoulders slightly to lead the viewer into the photo.

"SLIM AND STREAMLINED" POSE, STEP BY STEP

Turn your body at a 45-degree angle to the camera:
Option 1: Place your weight on your front foot,
bending your back leg slightly.
Option 2: Place your weight on your back foot,
and showcase your front foot.
Option 3: Distribute your weight evenly but
make sure you are sideways.

Draw upwards, creating a nice posture.

Look at your arms-
are they pressed against your sides?
Make sure your arms are away from
your body slightly so they appear as thin as possible.
Make sure you always have your arms
bent as this creates the nicest shape for a photograph.

Finally, look at the photographer and smile
or relax your face, depending on what mood you would like to
evoke.

BEFORE: Daena has her body facing forward in this photo. Unfortunately, it is not an engaging stance.
It's a pity this pretty girl is not going to attract any attention with this body language.

AFTER: (opposite page) Daena places her weight on her front foot and bends her back leg slightly. Photogenic success! Also, Daena's hand is on her hip. It's a great trick to keep her arms away from her body and bent to showcase them in the best possible way.

BEFORE: Chloe has her body facing forward and it is very unflattering. This is a thin, attractive girl but her knees are looking lumpy and her body language is awkward.

AFTER: Chloe places her weight on her back foot and showcases her front foot. Now she looks great. Also, the way Chloe has pointed her front foot keeps the entire pose very sophisticated.

BEFORE: With his body facing forward and his hands behind his back, Alex appears to lack confidence. His body language suggests he hates having his picture taken.

AFTER: Now that he has distributed his weight evenly and remained sideways, Alex looks confident. And confidence is attractive! Putting his hand in his hip pocket is a great way to make sure his arm is away from his body- giving him the most flattering arms possible.

21 / SLIM AND STREAMLINED POSE

FRAME IT

I imagine there are people out there who are just born photogenic. They wine and dine with naturally athletic people and perhaps enjoy chilling out with naturally gifted musicians.

Nice for them- but for me, I need to work the camera. If I did not create my "Frame it" pose I would look more insecure in photos. Luckily, I created this pose so I could appear confident and secure, and by teaching this pose I have helped countless others to appear that way, too. I honestly can say I use all the tools in this book to create nice pictures of myself, highlighting the positives and drawing attention away from the negatives.

As I said, when I was younger I was insecure about my teeth. I would tilt my head in an uncomfortable position. Another pose I would do was putting my hand over my mouth. There is not too much evidence of this as my family would plead for me to stop looking silly- so I uncomfortably removed my hand from my mouth and resumed the head tilt! Unfortunately, as a result, I was hiding my best asset because I was so focused on hiding my teeth. By head tilting, or covering my mouth, I was covering my nice, naturally full lips.

By resting my hands delicately by my side and giving a cheeky smile with my mouth closed, I attract attention to my lips while hiding my teeth. (They have since had braces, but old habits die slowly-it took years to finally smile!)

Our hands are our frames. They direct where people's eyes should go. Have you ever seen a newly presented car being showcased? The girl stands next to the car. She lifts the veil and then with her hands directs the viewers' attention to the car. This is what you are going to do for yourself.

No matter how relaxed your face and posture are, your hands will 'show' tension. Can you imagine a beautiful wedding photo, with you gazing into your partner's eyes, being ruined by the simple fact your hand is clenched?

24

It's easy to forget, but make sure your hands are relaxed. Even if you feel nervous you can look as calm as the ocean just by relaxing your hands.

Please note: Other people will look at your photo for no more than ten seconds. You are the only one who will sit there scrutinising yourself. And you can direct where you would like people's attention to go for that ten seconds. So lead them to your best assets!

If we work out what areas we don't like, we can make sure we don't cover those areas with our hands in photos. Doing that just showcases to everyone the parts we don't like. Take your hands away from your stomach or mouth, and stop clenching them!

A person who highlights with their hands what they love or like about themselves causes other people to notice these things as well. Your choosing to focus on the positive will encourage others to focus on those positives as well. It sounds crazy but it's true.

So let us distract attention away from our not-so-nice bits while highlighting what we find positive about ourselves, so others will notice, too.

"FRAME IT" POSE. STEP BY STEP

Before you attempt this pose find one asset you like about yourself. It may be your hair, your arms, your eyes. Also, make sure you know what you don't like, as you may be using your hands to cover this area when a camera presents itself.

Take a standing or seated position that you would like to be photographed in.

Draw upwards, creating a nice posture.

Make sure your arms are away from your body, reducing their width.

Take a nice deep breath.
As you breathe out, imagine all the tension leaving your body.

Frame your best asset with your hands. Just have them showcasing what you would like others to focus on.
Make sure your fingers are close together and your hands are looking relaxed.

Finally, look at the photographer and smile, or relax your face, depending on what mood you would like to evoke.

BEFORE: Chloe has crossed her arms across her stomach. This is a common mistake.

It causes the viewer to focus on exactly what Chloe is trying to hide, that she is self concious and does not want her picture taken.

AFTER: Wow, what a transformation! Chloe decides to showcase her best asset by bringing her hands to her hair. By doing this our eyes go directly to her hair and focus on what she likes best about herself.

27/ FRAME IT

BEFORE: Alex having his hands in a claw-like grip with each pose is an example of negative body language.

AFTER: When Alex rests his hands on his neck he draws attention to his torso. It's a very good place to direct attention for a masculine, confident look. And kudos for the other hand travelling down to the hip pocket, stopping it from becoming a tense claw.
A photogenic 10 out of 10 for this image!

BEFORE: As you can see, the hands across Diana's face and the lack of eye contact create a distant image.
It may feel comfortable for her, because she may be self-concious about her nose or smile, but no one will ever connect with her image.

AFTER: By showcasing her great eyes, Diana has everyone engaged, and keeps the viewers' focus on the windows to her soul.

YOUR NOSE IS A MAGNET

Many photographers have different theories on how to hold your head in a picture. A very famous male fashion photographer insisted his models lift their heads a little. This gives a very sensual and empowered look. Another well-known family portrait photographer likes people to lower their heads just a little to open up their eyes.

I can see good reasons why both these photographers swear by their head posing tricks. However, without all the fashion and glamour trimmings, the first pose can make a person look very arrogant, not mysterious. The second requires a huge amount of retouching effort. If we lower our face it will showcase any sagging skin around the two skin folds that run from each side of the nose. And thanks to Mother Nature, this can start to become an issue from as early as 30!

So a good way to pose is one that won't make it look like you're trying too hard, or make you cringe and reach for Photoshop. When somebody is taking a picture of you, it's best to have your face as centred as possible. Do not tilt your face dramatically in any fashion. Once you centre your face, all your features will fall into their most flattering position.

I imagine my nose has a magnet that wants to draw itself towards the camera lens, which I imagine has an even bigger magnet on the end of it. This allows the face to centre nicely and come forward slightly.

As the face draws itself towards the lens it eradicates double chins, if you have any. Make sure you don't draw it too far forward or you may look a little strange. You will know when you have gone too far as you will find it difficult to smile because you are uncomfortable. Also, when centreing your face towards the camera do not bring out the measuring tape! Your face often will have a slight tilt or angle to it. Angles are nice, and complement facial features, in moderation.

The next issue is what mood you would like to evoke. Once you have your face in place you can either smile confidently, or relax the face and give a closed-mouth, cheeky grin while smiling with your eyes. Or perhaps give a strong look that requires no smiling.

But how do you "smile with your eyes" you ask?

Focus the attention on one particular cheek. Imagine you are lifting the cheek up as you give your cheeky, one-sided grin. What will happen is your eyes will kick slightly into a "happy grin mode." Your lips with every smile will curve slightly upwards.

To give a confident smile imagine winning the lotto, playing with your children, or the photographer in funny underpants (Who cares? It works!). To just pretend to smile looks fake and you will come across as false in your photos. You actually have to imagine something that will make you smile. (Unless you are being photographed at a fabulous party, you have had some champagne already, and are smiling happily anyway!)

A strong look is powerful and can work wonders if it is executed correctly. When you look at the photographer, breathe ever so slightly out of your nose. This stops your face from tensing up and keeps it cool and strong, instead of tense and angry. It is a big difference, and one we want to get right.

"YOUR NOSE IS A MAGNET" POSE. STEP BY STEP

Stand or sit in the pose you would like to be photographed in.

Draw upwards, creating a nice posture.

Make sure your arms are away from your body, reducing their width.

Take a nice deep breath.
As you breathe out, imagine all the tension leaving your body.

Check that your hands are positioned nicely, showing no tension.

Look to where the photographer is standing.
Imagine your nose is a magnet and is attracted to the centre of the lens.
Wherever the photographer moves the camera, your nose follows.

Finally, don't forget to smile, or relax your face and smile with your eyes, or look strong and cool,
depending on what mood you would like to evoke.

BEFORE: Daena is stretching her eyes to reach the camera lens. Her lips are tightly closed, which makes her appear tight-lipped.

AFTER: By turning her head to meet the camera lens, Daena's eyes are bright and centred. Her beautiful smile beams at the viewer. I am sure Deana is thinking of something that makes her happy.

A perfect and inviting photograph.

BEFORE: Alex is stretching his eyes to reach the camera lens. His mouth expression is not convincing. When you are giving a "smile with the eyes," you need to have confidence- or it will be mistaken for a grimace.

AFTER: Alex turns his head to meet the camera lens. His facial features are even and centred.
By just lifting the cheek a little on his left side he gives a convincing smile with his eyes.

BEFORE: Diana is stretching her eyes to reach the camera lens. By not having her face forward whilst not smiling she gives off a scheming vibe.

Diana must centre her face if she wants to pull off this strong but cool look.

AFTER: Diana turns her head to meet the camera lens. Her facial features are even and centred. Diana has a strong look that is not tense because she is breathing out slowly from her nose- which relaxes her face.

$\mathscr{S}$TITCHING

ow we have covered photogenic tips and tricks from tip to toe. No part of the body lacks a pose. But to seal the deal on your new photogenic quest, you need to master what I have named "Stitching."

Have you ever held your pose while the photographer takes four or five photographs? Do you know what happens? You actually start to look stiff. In actual fact, you can really only hold a pose for ten seconds. After that the pose becomes false and you are ready for the pose to be over.

Stitching is essentially moving between two variations of the same pose. It is moving just enough to refresh your stance, but not so much that the camera picks up movement.

For example, it would be very hard to move from a seated pose to a standing one, or vice versa, without it being noticed. So instead, keep the same pose, but just move your arm and hand into different positions. This allows your images to stay fresh, and you start looking like a superstar or supermodel.

Don't forget to hold each pose for ten seconds, allowing the photographer to capture you. Also, I would add two different emotions to each pose. This gives your different facial muscles a break, as holding one emotion (such as a wide smile) can start to give you sore cheeks and stop you from looking as though you are truly happy.

For example, the first pose could be you with a lovely laugh, standing in the slim and streamlined pose with your arm resting on your leg (bent and away from your body, remember!). After holding that pose for ten seconds, just move the arm up on your hip and give a more serious look, or a cheeky grin.

Another example is looking at the camera with a warm smile, then looking away and gazing out at the sunset/park/window, relaxing your face and looking more serious.

"STITCHING" POSE. STEP BY STEP

Stand or sit in the pose you would like to be photographed in.

Draw upwards, creating a nice posture.

Make sure your arms are away from your body- reducing their width.

Take a nice deep breath.
As you breathe out, imagine all the tension leaving your body.

Check that your hands are positioned nicely, showing no tension.

Centre your face as if your nose is a magnet attracted to the middle of the lens.

Hold the position for ten seconds.
Then slowly move into another, slightly different position.
Blink and relax your face while you do so.
Hold the position for ten seconds.
Slowly move back into the original position you held.
Keep repeating until the photographer is happy they got a great shot.

POSE 1: Chloe is posing in the "Slim and streamlined" pose with her hand on her hip. She is giving a strong but cool look to the camera.

POSE 2: Chloe keeps her "Slim and streamlined" pose, and only changes which hand rests on the hip. She also is combining her favourite "Frame it" pose by tucking some hair behind her ear whilst smiling.
A wonderful example of "Stitching".

POSE 1: Mitch is posing in a "Frame it" pose. By resting his hands on his chin, Mitch is directing attention towards his facial features.

POSE 2: A great tip for people who are nervous and can't think of a second pose- look down or away. This can create a great "moody" look whilst also allowing you to refresh your facial features and blink your eyes. Mitch has utilised this trick to create a great second image. If he had stayed in the original pose he would have become stiff and the image would not have looked natural.

POSE 1: Diana is in the "Slim and streamlined" pose.
A beautiful, fresh smile also gives the pose a light and happy feeling.

POSE 2: Diana has used a great trick. She adjusted her mood when she adjusted her feet whilst maintaining the "Streamlined" pose. Diana now has turned the look into a more cool and strong image.

But inside movement there is one moment at which the elements in motion are in balance. Photography must seize upon this moment and hold immobile the equilibrium of it.

Henri Cartier-Bresson

POSING WITH OTHERS

As I am writing this chapter it is summertime in Sydney. As Sydney is in the southern hemisphere, we have a warm Christmas and New Year's. And it was the best one I have ever had. Between the alfresco Christmas seafood family lunches, the Sydney Fireworks display and playing in the backyard with my baby girl- I lived through many moments I will cherish forever. And with these moments and celebrations there are group photographs that need to be taken.

I will not forget this Christmas, when I announced that we must take a family portrait with everyone included. Most of our neighbours were out at family lunches. After many door knocks I politely but firmly dragged a neighbour out of his house and onto our front lawn to be the photographer. He was vacuuming up after his family lunch and had no shirt on. There were giggles amongst my family as they know how far I will go to get a family memory captured.

Group photographs are great because they usually are taken at a special function or party. So they really do become special. The first issue with group photographs is that a small gap between people actually can appear quite large in a photograph. This can appear as people seeming distant and slightly cold. The first step you need to take is closing the gap. If you are not very close just make sure you stand close, but there's no need to interlink arms. If you look at celebrity "Are they together? Are they not?" articles they always plaster them with a photograph of the couple at a celebrity function standing together with a big gap in between them. Celebrity couples always are told by their publicists to stand together or it could be interpreted as being too cold with one another. The media can pick up on that and create a news story just from body language in a photograph. It must be very stressful being a celebrity couple.

However, if you are more like me and take pictures at family functions, not of celebrities on the red carpet, then make sure there is a closer connection. Placing hands around each other is nice. Resting your hands on someone else's shoulder is great as

54

well. This makes you appear close and happy. But don't forget to relax those hands!

The second issue with group poses is blinking. With large groups you tend to get someone blinking in nearly all of the shots. If there is a general party atmosphere then ask everyone to close their eyes. Then the photographer can say "One...two...three... open." This allows everyone to open their eyes at once and you have a perfect group photo with everyone looking fresh-faced and wide-eyed.

Another great tip is to make sure everyone is grouped along an invisible straight line. Ensure the group does not create a semi-circle. Why? Because then the people on each end of the semi-circle will appear larger. This is due to them being closer to the camera. Sometimes it can be quite dramatic and they can have a body that looks twice as big as the person standing in the middle of the circle. If you cannot control the group and it is naturally forming a semi-circle please make sure you are not on either end. Place yourself in the most flattering position- the middle.

If you are a close group of friends and you know in advance you would like your group photo taken then perhaps you could coordinate outfits. There is no need to go overboard but just note that patterns are okay – in moderation!
Patterns can add visual interest and texture as well as a good dose of personality. If someone insists on wearing their favourite patterned dress, just make sure the rest of the subjects are in simple, more solid colour pieces.
Avoid anything with logos, graphics, characters, and labels. Also avoid clothes that are incredibly trendy right now that may appear dated in the next five to ten years.
For example, I always used to wear trendy things when I was younger, in the 1990s. I insisted on wearing the coolest threads to every group get together. I wore things like my:

-Hypercolor purple and yellow florescent t-shirt with "HYPERCOLOR" written all over the front.
-A shirt with a cartoon of a celery stick with eyes on a surfboard saying "Psychedelic waves, man".

Wow- how dated are those photographs! Great for a laugh but, needless to say, Mum never put them on the mantelpiece.

But once I wore a white dress and a denim jacket. I still dressed within the 1990s fashion but the image did not look as dated. Just my head tilting!
The whites-and-denim look still looks great today. Denim cuts and washes change, but rarely do they become dated (with the exception of the matching denim jacket top and pants, ouch!)

Don't forget, if it is a fun group shot- props that blend with the vibe of the session can be meaningful and fun. A vintage camera or fedora can bring instant fun to the portrait.

Stand together in a group.

If you are a work group, stand close while remaining comfortable.

If you are close to one another, link arms and place a hand on each other's shoulders.

Make sure your arms are away from your body, reducing their width, as group shots can make you feel like you are squished and you may push your arms in.

Have the photographer instruct everyone to close their eyes.

Have the photographer instruct the group to open their eyes on the camera click.

Once the more formal photograph is taken some candids can be captured.

This is a great time to introduce props, or just have everyone laughing and interacting.

Keep repeating until the photographer is happy they got a great shot.

POSE 1: The group looks distant and far apart.

POSE 2: The group looks like they are having fun and are close.

$\mathscr{S}$ELFIES

The wonderful attribute of the "selfie" is the photographer (you) has absolute control of what gets shared and what gets deleted. As someone who was very shy once, I could understand if you may not feel comfortable practicing my poses with a friend, partner, or family member for fear of seeming too narcissistic or not looking good on camera.

Selfies allow you to open up and capture yourself without being embarrassed. No one else is there to say "Haven't we taken enough images of you?" So this is a great opportunity to capture some of the most open and honest pictures of who you think you are.

I am a strong believer in the power of an image. If you capture a positive image of yourself, it becomes your own personal cheerleader and positive reinforcement. You will be unstoppable.

I have given you tips and tricks on how to look fabulous in photographs. However, the next important stage is how to make a photograph into one that has an X-factor. So follow these tips below.

TIP #1: YOUR LOOK

Your look is very important. Your collection of "selfies" that you share with others will start to give an overall message about who you are. Are you a book worm who loves crazy glasses? Or perhaps a party person who is always snapping himself (or herself) looking fabulous? Capture who you are.

The important message I am getting across is you must have elements that are uniquely you and fun. Otherwise, your identity will get lost in the white fuzz. I get tired of seeing selfies of people showcasing their breakfast, drinking their twentieth cocktail, or walking their pet.

I love seeing people share their passion for wearing vintage hats and scarfs. I enjoy selfies that proudly showcase the person's amazing ability to create a Michelin Star dish. You already will have a unique style. I would add this to your selfies. It will give your online personally a more unique twist. Make your images count by making them unique to your individual style or lifestyle.

TIP #2: YOUR LIGHT

When I teach my workshop "How to Look Good in Photos," I always ask this question:

"If I said I wanted to take a photo of you right now. Where would you stand?"

Everyone in my class always starts looking around the room for a clean wall or nice backdrop for their image. This is a constant in my class. But, unfortunately, it is a constant mistake. Never search for the backdrop. Search for the best light. A backdrop can be cropped out. Unflattering shadows under your eyes are harder to remove.

The most important trick for any amazing photo is even light. If you only take one piece of advice from this book do not forget the following:

AN EVEN LIGHT CAN MAKE YOU APPEAR FIVE YEARS YOUNGER INSTANTLY.
IT CAN REDUCE BLEMISHES, AND SMOOTH SKIN.
EVEN LIGHT IS YOUR NEW BEST FRIEND.

What happens is if a light source is not even across your face, blemishes and wrinkles create darker shadows. This makes them more obvious and I have yet to meet someone who likes having more obvious lines and blemishes on their face. Also, please remember that florescent light seems to make you look five to ten years older, especially when you are photographed under it.

When you face straight on to a light source it will illuminate the skin and blast wrinkles and blemishes from view. Please note that wrinkles and blemishes are not as obvious as the shadows they create. So if we eradicate the shadows with an even, natural light we reduce the appearance of wrinkles.

I once taught a client this handy tip and she was amazed. She since has reported that even when she dines at restaurant she always tries to sit in the chair that is directly facing a window so her face is filled with natural light. She calls it her mini-facelift trick--and it is such a wonderful secret to know that I don't blame her.

TIP #3: YOUR LOCATION

This tip does not mean your actual physical location, but the location of your camera lens. Obviously, because a selfie is a quick and fun image, the camera or smartphone will be held in your own hands. So two things we need to avoid when holding the camera on our own are double chins and nostrils.

Remember my "your nose is a magnet" pose? Well, this is a very important tip to remember when taking a selfie. Raise your arm, then draw your face towards the camera lens so your chin will be its leanest. But do not lift your face too high or you will be showcasing your nostrils -- and who wants a nostril selfie!

Another option when taking a selfie is cropping in on your face quite closely .
This cuts out your arm from the frame. Draw your face towards the lens. This type of selfie will showcase your eyes incredibly. The great thing about a selfie is you can take a series of images without too much effort. Delete what you don't like and share your favourite one.

Emma has added an interesting vintage hat to make her look unique. By adding fun accessories the image has a more standout quality. The first image shows how Emma is positioning the camera and the second image demonstrates how her face would be framed in a selfie.

In the first image we can see Emma is directly facing her light source. This allows for a very flattering photograph which reduces blemishes and naturally smooths skin. The second and third images demonstrate how flattering this type of selfie can be for the eyes.

In photography there are no shadows that cannot be illuminated.

Berenice Abbott

PROFESSIONAL PHOTOGRAPHS

*I*n this world we are all "Googled." But for some reason, people assume this is something that takes place after you have met someone socially. But today, most of your potential employers are doing a little background research on you before you even turn up for your first round of interviews.

Imagine all those nerves you feel when you arrive at your first job interview. In your head you are presenting yourself for the first time to a panel of interviewers. However, most of them probably have seen your professional online C.V. and potentially your main image on any social media networking page.

TIP #1: YOUR LOOK

First of all, analyse the professional pictures you have online at the moment. Did a colleague snap a quick picture standing against your office wall for your networking page? Was it in the afternoon when you were not at your prime?

I constantly am surprised at what people have put on their professional corporate networking page. I have seen photographs where the person clearly is tired and not into having their photo taken. You need to ask yourself this question: Would you turn up to a job interview looking unimpressed?

I would keep your look professional and confident. An easy way to create this is to wear a suit. Both men and women always look like they are about to wheel and deal when they are in a suit. Often you won't see the entire suit as professional images are rarely full body shots. But to dress in the whole outfit allows you to have confidence and makes you feel powerful from the feet up.

To add some confidence to your photograph please stand in my "slim and streamlined" pose if you are standing. And if you are sitting or standing make sure you utilise my "your nose is a magnet" pose. This allows you to have a confident look. Also, this is the only appropriate time that you can cross your arms.

Any other time would seem like you're just hiding your stomach. However, in this situation it looks very powerful.

TIP #2: YOUR LIGHT

As I mentioned earlier, when you face straight on to a light source, light will then illuminate the skin and blast wrinkles and blemishes from view. So keep the light flattering. However, in regards to light, nine times out of ten you will get a reflection if you wear glasses. Especially if you are facing a natural light source like a window. Your eyes get lost behind the glare.

One professional piece of advice: If you wear glasses now is the time to utilise them as a prop. People always assume you are so much more intelligent when you wear glasses. I am not sure as to why--it seems we just make that connection. I wear glasses for reading but my brother, who is studying for his Ph.D. at the most prestigious cancer research facility in Australia, does not need glasses at all. However, I could put money down that he has a higher IQ than me. But aside from reality, glasses make a good impression.

So take photographs of yourself as if you are just taking your glasses off. That way you get the best of both worlds. You get the smart aspect and you showcase your eyes.

TIP #3: YOUR LOCATION

The location of the camera is directly in front of you. This professional image must not be a "selfie"-type image. You can have a friend or a colleague hold the camera. Just make sure you take it earlier on in the day before the wind has been taken out of your sails. Stay looking fresh.

Even if you are like me and work in the creative field and find no reason to have a Forbes-type photo shoot--why not do it just for fun? It may be good for your confidence. You don't have to show anyone. Just have a glance at it before you go into any negotiation. No matter how creative your field, we all have to negotiate. So make sure you can visualise yourself as that powerhouse of confidence.

BEFORE: Giles has his body facing forward and it is very unflattering. The overhead office lights also are causing very strong shadows under his hairline.

AFTER: Giles places his weight on his back foot and creates a confident stance. Now he looks great. Also, by standing in a doorway of his office building he allows natural light to be even across his face.

BEFORE: Emma has quite severe window glare in her glasses. This covers her eyes, which are an important feature in a flattering photograph.

AFTER: Emma poses holding her glasses. This indicates she wears them often but also allows for her eyes to be showcased.

DATING PROFILE PHOTOGRAPHS

*C*an I just say here and now that I love taking photographs of clients for their dating profiles? I am not a very good matchmaker, so this is my chance to help people find true love. And who doesn't love doing that?

It is always the same way. A potential client calls asking for photographs, sounding slightly more nervous than usual.

Client: "Ummm...Hi...I would like to get some pictures for ummm...me. Yes, just for me..."
Me: "That's great. Could I just ask what you will be using them for so I can talk about styling with you? Are they for work, or family, or I have a lot of clients having their picture taken for dating profiles?"
Client: "Really? Yes? Others do it? Yes, it's for dating. I want to try online dating."
Me: "Well done for taking the first step. Your photograph is your shop window and by having a good image you ultimately will produce better results."

So read on and learn the tips and tricks necessary for the best dating profile images.

TIP #1: YOUR LOOK

Your profile needs to stand out. It does that by showing attractive and good quality photographs of you. However, you not only want to attract attention with a great photograph, but also communicate who you are to attract the right suitor.

Dress for your dating profile images as if you were dressing for your dream partner. Are you a person who loves to laugh? Show that in your photographs. Or perhaps you are more sophisticated and love the finer things in life--dress to impress.

This group of fun images definitely showcased Giles love of a good laugh. Using a prop like sunglasses allows you to make a story out of your images and express a sense of fun.

These images show Giles to be more sophisticated, without seeming too corporate. By placing him in an elegant setting he looks more relaxed and a lover of the finer things in life. By using the "your nose is a magnet" pose he can sit in a relaxed position away from the camera, but still remain photogenic.

When advertisers create a scene for a photo shoot they always take into consideration their target market. And you essentially are aiming to appeal to your dream partner, that's your target market. There is no point in just posting an attractive photo with no insight into who you are. Do you want quality or quantity? I certainly think quality is the best way to go. You will at least enjoy meeting all these different people who have similar interests. People sometimes say, "But isn't that what the text part of the profile is for?" My response is: "Have you ever flicked through a magazine looking at all the different product ads? If so, do you ever remember saying, 'Wow, what an amazing paragraph of product text!'?" I doubt it. The only thing that grabs your attention is the advertising image. Your profile text is fine print compared to your photograph. People will react first to your photograph.

TIP #2: YOUR LIGHT

Once again, do not forget the number one rule about lighting. When you face straight on to a light source, then light will illuminate the skin and blast wrinkles and blemishes from view.

The only difference with dating profiles is sometimes the images will be taken outdoors. If you are a sporty person you obviously may want to capture yourself in great active gear with a beautiful location in the background. Hey, who would not want to date you then!

So when you are outdoors, please remember the sun can be a harsh friend at times. If the stunning backdrop only offers you harsh sun on your face, then close your eyes and when the self-timer or your friend taking the shot indicates it's time to smile, only then open your eyes. That will give the best result. If the sun is too harsh for you then gaze out towards the landscape. This still will say a lot about who you are, but you will not be able to make this your main profile shot. It will just add to your enticing story. It still will be worth adding. Trust me.

TIP #3: YOUR LOCATION

For these types of images the camera needs to be in the hands of a close friend. Remember how I said dress for your dating profile images as if you were dressing for your dream weekend with your partner? Well, there is no point dressing up in active wear and taking the image in your kitchen! You actually have to venture outside to where you would jog, walk the dog, or power walk.

When you are outdoors or sitting in a cafe you do not want to spend hours leaning the camera against a rock or a salt shaker. It will be very hard to prop up a camera, put on the self-timer and then pose. It may take hours. So get a close friend to hold your camera or smartphone to make life a little easier, and the day more fun.

Just let your friend know how important light is. That way they can make sure your face is in even light, or instruct you when to open your eyes if the sun is a little harsh. So get out there and make some images and have a laugh!

Embrace light. Admire it. Love it. But above all, know light. Know it for all you are worth, and you will know the key to photography.

George Eastman

Posing With Kids

*H*ave you ever been in negotiations with a child? It's one of the toughest negotiations out there, especially when you want them to smile for the camera. Often when I am in a cafe I watch a mother trying to capture a moment with frustration written all over her face. Their gorgeous child will have milk froth on their upper lip and it is definitely "a Kodak moment." The mother is begging her child to look up at the camera. But the kid has cottoned on and won't have a bar of it.

Mother: "Please look at the camera, Charlotte. Mummy wants the photo."
Child: "No. I DOOOOON'T WANT TOOOOO."

Kodak moment over.

The most important thing to remember is if the child is under five years old you have ten minutes to get a photo before they are over it. If they are over five you have twenty minutes. That's it. That's all you got.

Please don't forget that kids don't need to smile all the time. Sometimes if they are interested in something the most stunning, serene look washes over their faces. Capture that, too.

TIP #1: YOUR LOOK

I have a great tip. Walk around your home and note the décor colours in each room. There may be a predominate theme or standout one-off pieces. Next, go to your children's wardrobe and coordinate outfits that would blend with different parts of the décor. Have your children wear these outfits at your mini photo shoot.

Once you print and hang the photographs it will look as though you hired a stylist to coordinate the entire project. They will have a beautiful harmony to them and certainly will make the memory special.

TIP #2: YOUR LIGHT

The one thing I love about children is their ability to throw a tantrum the minute they are over a situation. And one thing that irritates a child most is glare and heat.

As an adult you may deal with the harsh sun because that's your only option for the shot. But kids never will want a bar of it. The main rule with lighting for children is keep them in the most neutral light possible to avoid agitation. Keep them happy and they should keep smiling. Well, at least for 10-20 minutes.

TIP #3: YOUR LOCATION

My suggestion is tell the photographer or family member taking the photo to hide the camera and try to focus on engaging the child first. Let's say your husband is taking the photo, and you are the photographic assistant. Play your kids' favourite music in the background. Then when they are laughing and enjoying themselves bring out the camera and capture the moment.

BOOM--photo magic.

Sophia is listening to a fun children's song and she is clearly very happy and enjoying the song. The lighting is very neutral so not to cause any glare in her eyes. Also, after the song Sophia started looking out the window, and even though she is not smiling, it is still a beautiful shot.

In nature, light creates the color. In the picture, color creates the light.

Hans Hofmann

THE CAMERA CONNECTION

J am sure you have reached this part of the book and thought, "Okay, so I have to stand slightly to the side, face the camera, frame my assets, utilise stitching, pre-empt my look, organise the light source, and do all this to music. That's a lot. Thanks, Kate." You're probably thinking...

Will most photographs allow time for all this?
And won't every photograph look the same?

My answer to you is this: Do you remember driving lessons? At first you were so conscious about switching on the car, backing out of the drive and clicking on the indicator. You had to process where the window wipers were and you got a little anxious at intersections. Now I am sure you just hop in your car and drive. Your only concern is the other cars and your route. The rest is on automatic pilot.

If you practise in the mirror at home or, better yet, taking selfies with the automatic timer, all these tips and tricks will become natural to you. When you see a camera you automatically will frame your features and turn slightly to the side. Occasionally there will be times when the group shot is taken in an instant and all you can do is move closer and face the camera directly. Or if your partner captures you in front of a monument that is crowded and you only have a few seconds, you may just remember to move your arms away from your body. You cannot have every shot perfect every time. That would be boring!

However, each person will have one particular trick they will need to utilise in every photo. If you have a double chin then "Your nose is a magnet pose" is essential in every photograph. If you are a bit cuddly it may be important to make sure your arms are away from your body in every shot.

But in regards to each photograph looking the same, don't worry. That never will happen. The camera will be at different angles, capturing different moments. It rarely will be the same. A perfect example is the cover photo of my book. This was taken by my husband at one of our favourite holiday destinations in the Blue Mountains not far from Sydney.

Every time we visit I always comment about how dramatic the landscape is. We stay in a country cottage and watch the thunderstorms brew with the windmills turning and the crickets screeching. Cue opera music, please.

So, being me, I once brought two dresses on a particular weekend stay. One, for me, I had received as a gift from a close friend, and the other was for my daughter. I wanted a photograph of us girls frolicking in this picturesque landscape. It was going to be such a great shot.

My husband is not a trained photographer but he had my professional camera and we were laughing and taking pictures of me and my daughter. Sophia decided she did not want to participate anymore (our ten minutes were up), and instead pulled at the long country grass like a normal two-year-old would. We declared the photo shoot over and went about running around, acting silly.

I probably was running after Sophia in this photo and my husband said, "Turn around." And so I just automatically made sure I was slightly side-on and I turned my face as much as I could, imaging my nose was a magnet attracted to the camera lens--and I smiled.

And that's what happens--you make a connection. This connection goes beyond conscious processing. Your body develops a memory in the same way your arms automatically reach out to catch a ball. Your body moves into the right place when you see a camera. The camera connection.

Trust me. One day you will see.

This image was taken outdoors. I imagined I just automatically made sure I was slightly side-on and I turned my face as much as I could, imaging my nose was a magnet attracted to the camera lens--and I smiled.

RETOUCHING IS EVERYWHERE

I once read an article about the perils of retouching. It was written by a very "anti-retouching," "anti-advertising" guru. This writer made out that using retouching tools was a slippery slope to plastic surgery. Ironically, this writer had her blog photo next to the article. It was an image taken with a smartphone with a retro filter applied to it.

Do you know why people love taking smartphone selfies with a filter added to them? When we use smartphone filters we are putting our photograph through a process which throws information away. We reduce the amount of dark and light areas to create a smoother and more pleasant image.

Do you know why people love retouching? When we retouch a photograph we remove information (wrinkles, blemishes, freckles). Every time you are using a filter program, app, or plug-in you are essentially retouching your face.

Bottom line: Basic retouching can create beautiful images. And I personally do not want a world full of average images. Do you? I am a lover of art and design and I expect a nice chair to have a smooth finish. So why not a picture?

I am lucky enough to have witnessed the changes photography has undertaken within my 12-year career. I studied photo media at university where I had the benefit of being educated in digital and film photography. I was nineteen when I started university in 2000. I was one of the last classes to be taught film basics.

With my film training I learnt the retouching basics that still apply today. We always would retouch faces in the dark room. As the image was hitting the photographic paper we would block harsh shadows under the eye area and banish blemishes so the portrait appeared more flattering.

As a portrait photographer I used a medium-format Hasselblad camera with a film back before I switched to my Canon digital camera. When my clients were posed in beautiful, even, natural light I would use E6 film (slide film) but process it as C41 (standard film). This would push the vibrancy and allow the colours to sing, stand out and look spectacular. Removing the information made the skin appear smooth and refreshed. Photographers called this technique "cross processing." Filters in retouching programs, smartphone apps and plug-ins create a similar effect today.

So let's face it- retouching is everywhere. And it is becoming more and more a part of everyday life. So we need to understand it. People believe retouching is an evil sin that started with Adobe Photoshop. Yes, advertisers take it too far and, yes, it can do harm. But a moderate amount of editing can add to a photograph's beauty. And yours!

99/ Retouching is Everywhere

BEFORE: This image of Chloe has had no filter added to the image. The colours are quite bland and lack energy.

AFTER: The portrait of Chloe is much more vibrant when a filter (similar to the cross processing technique) is added.

THE 10 PERCENT

hen it comes to retouching it is important not to throw the baby out with the bath water. Retouching has its positives, yes indeed. Retouching is great for removing blemishes, dark circles, stray hairs, food stains on clothes or lipstick on teeth. The important rule to remember is other people will not flinch if you improve your appearance by 10 percent. However, if you morph into another person, then people are going to notice.

So why not make your C.V. image, dating profile, or Christmas card its visual best? Go for it, but understand there are rules. To get that job, that date, or that genuineness, your photo needs to be retouched no more than 10 percent. Retouching is like red wine. A little is very nice, but have too much and you will look like a fool.

Many magazine brands do a great job at taking a good looking woman and turning her into an unnatural looking being. I find it funny when a celebrity cover model has had her eye balls and teeth retouched and whitened to the extreme. It turns a very attractive woman into an alien.

Just remember any retouching that includes shaving down hips or creating unreal cheekbones will cause you future grief. Our unique structure must not be tampered with. People unconsciously scan our facial and bodily architecture. So if you have decided to create thinner hips and a smaller nose you probably will begin to look like a stranger.

A great tip is that filters on smartphone apps do the perfect amount of retouching. It's simple, costs hardly anything and you can look great in less than two minutes. And I would prefer to use a filter to look better rather than manually reducing dark circles or bad lighting. I would find sitting down and spending hours on my photographs a little boring and a waste of my already precious time.

Have you ever been out to a picnic in the afternoon light and started falling in love with how everything looks in the beautiful sunset? That warm light that just makes everything look romantic and special? Well, you can wait until 6 p.m. to capture your memories or just choose a warm filter to create a similar effect. A plethora of filters can be used to accomplish this.

Every photo retouching program offers ready-made filters. Filters also are available as smartphone plug-ins or smartphone apps. They have different names but these are some of the more effective filters:

BLACK AND WHITE   PAPARAZZI
VINTAGE   BLEAR
RETRO   AMARO
CROSS PROCESS   MAYFAIR
MILK SKIN   RISE
VIVID   X-PRO
BABY FACE   TOASTER
LOMO-FI   SUNNY
AVENUE   GRACE
LUCKY   LOFT

To use these tools on your photo you first have to select the type of filter you would like to use. A series of filters usually appear and you can click on one of several potential filters and they will apply to your image straight away. Once you have chosen your preferred filter, select save, download or share.

The other tool that is great for removing blemishes, stray hairs, food or lipstick on teeth can go by the following names:

CLONE TOOL   MAGIC WAND
BLEMISH REMOVAL TOOL   RETOUCH TOOL

To use these tools on your photo you first have to open up your photo in the program. Then you select an icon. It usually appears as a small dot or paintbrush. Then you select the object you would like to remove. Once the blemish/lipstick mark has been selected with the tool it usually disappears. In more advanced programs you can choose what goes in its place. However, with smartphone retouching apps or plug-ins it will choose by itself.

If you are using a professional camera and don't want to put your image through a filter then you have other options as well. There are websites showcasing professional re-touchers from around the world who offer to retouch one or two photos for anything from $5- $25. Fiverr.com, Ebay.com, and Etsy.com are some examples. These re-touchers are happy to provide their C.V. and before and after examples.

A great tip is that re-touchers only need direction, payment and the photograph. The rest is up to them. After signing up to a site with reputable payment methods (I only pay via PayPal.) it's just a matter of picking your retouch artist.

To use these websites effectively, direct your retouch artist well. I strongly suggest giving clear instructions and offering a visual example. Just remember to keep the example in the context of what you want done. If you would like your dress to be more vivid and shadows on your face removed, then offer examples of that.

105/ THE 10 PERCENT

Here is a great portrait of Karim put through a series of filters. The filter throws information away, and reduces the amount of dark and light areas to create a smoother and more pleasant image.

$\mathcal{C}$ONCLUSION

I am sure the tips in this book will assist you in looking good in photos. I may even have made you a little excited about getting your picture taken. Please remember that practise makes perfect. You may feel a little silly at first, standing in front of a mirror creating my "Frame It" pose, or my "Slim and Streamlined" pose--but it all will be worth it.

In fact, that is exactly what the models and celebrities do. Nobody wakes up and just walks into a photo shoot and works the camera like a professional. Most celebrities have practised and practised their signature stances and poses in front of a mirror for hours.

Marilyn Monroe studied body posture for most of her career. She created her on-camera persona through sheer practise and determination. There is a famous book, *The Thinking Body* by Mabel Elsworth. This book defines posture and how it reflects who you are. Marilyn always believed beauty secrets should stay secret. However, she often was seen with this book. And you thought she just arrived into the world giggling and bouncing around with the greatest of ease.

My goal was to move beyond the dread of being in a photograph. I wanted to have beautiful family memories as they are very important to me. I clearly just wanted to progress from my camera shyness. Find your own level of investment and photogenic style.

One of my life-changing moments happened in a Sydney nursing home. I was finishing my Masters of Art Therapy at the University of Western Sydney. Art Therapy uses visual imagery as a language tool. As humans we were drawing before we were writing. This amazing degree made me understand the sheer power of a painting, photo, or drawing. From the art world, to the advertising world, to your own personal memories--images can story tell, convince, express and manipulate. And even though I have no desire to be a therapist, I had a desire to understand visual communication. Along with my academic research I was visiting nursing home patients weekly. I was looking though their albums and hearing their life stories for my practical component.

There were all different types of interesting people who had very different life experiences, from doctors who travelled the world researching to mothers who had raised children. Some had seen fame or had money--their career highlights and travel pictures filled their albums. Others may have had different successes documented in their photos. A gorgeous, chubby child's first walk, or eight grandchildren celebrating their grandfather's 80th birthday.

No matter what their life experience, photographs were all that were left. Accolades, travel, youth, the beauty of your baby--it all slips though what we call time. And I learnt that as you get older (if you are blessed to do so) your memory starts to become a little unreliable. But a photograph can remind you, bring a smile to your face, and take you back to that moment--even if just for a minute.

So stand in front of that camera and smile. The moment doesn't just require you to, your future does as well.

Made in the USA
San Bernardino, CA
21 June 2014